7/97

**Farmington Public
Library District**

266 East Fort Street
Farmington, Illinois 61531
(309) 245-2175

The Trouble with Uncle

First U.S. Edition

First published in Great Britain in 1992
by Heinemann Young Books

ISBN 0-316-15190-4

Library of Congress Catalog Card Number 91-40162
Library of Congress Cataloging-in-Publication
information is available.

10 9 8 7 6 5 4 3 2 1

Printed and bound in Italy
by L.E.G.O. S.p.A., Vicenza

ALSO BY BABETTE COLE
Hurray for Ethelyn

**To Alan, the coolest
skipper under the sun**

The Trouble with Uncle

Babette Cole

Little, Brown and Company
Boston Toronto London

The trouble
with Uncle is...

he doesn't just play around with boats . . . .

Uncle found his own club.

One of the members sold him a *real* treasure map.

"Come on. Now we can get rich quick!"
said Uncle.

Uncle tried to work out the way to the island,
but he couldn't do the math.

"Load of rubbish!" he said.
So we set sail anyway.

We were lost at sea for ages.

Eventually…
"Land ahoy!" shouted Uncle.

But when we dropped anchor,
the land started to move!

"Take that hook out of my nose at once!" said the whale. "And then I'll take you to your silly island."

We set off at top speed.

"Good riddance!" said the whale.

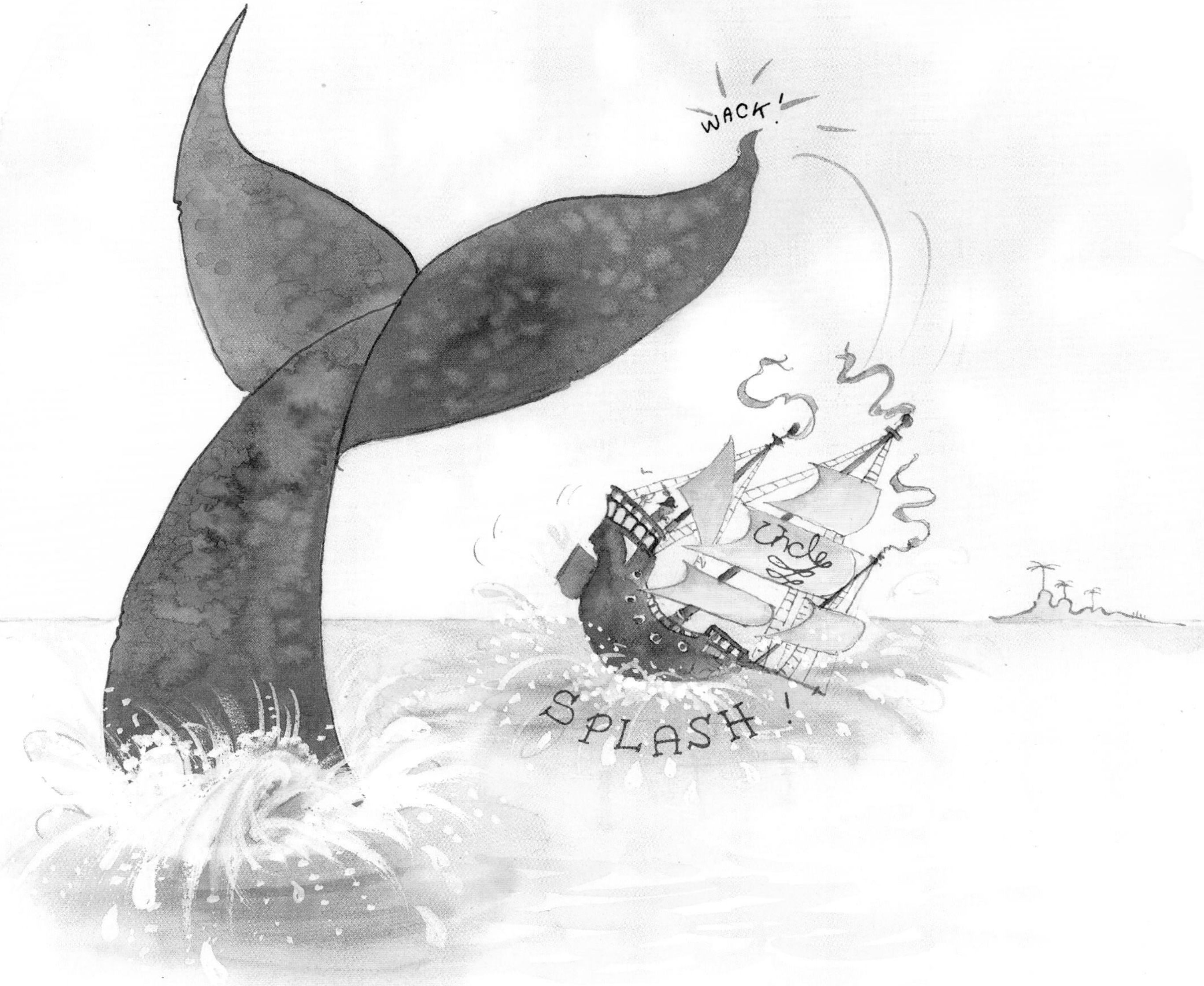

"This must be it," said Uncle.

It was the
right island,
of course.

But someone had built a hotel on top of the treasure.

The hotel was full of movie stars.

Then some real pirates came alongside.

They kidnapped Lovelace L'amour, the famous movie star, and took all her jewels.

Rescuing Lovelace was easy
for Uncle.

And the pirates left all her jewels behind.

She gave Uncle
a reward.

But back at sea it fell
overboard.

Luckily a mermaid
caught it.

She taught Uncle sailors' math.
Uncle fell in love!

They were married
by the parrot!

NAVIGATION
YACHTMASTER
TREASURE ISLAND
SEAMANSHIP

Sailing home was no
trouble at all.

But now I've got trouble with Aunty!